This Far Back Everything Shimmers

Vicki Husband

Vagabond Voices
Glasgow

© Vicki Husband 2016

First published in May 2016 by
Vagabond Voices Publishing Ltd.,
Glasgow,
Scotland.

ISBN 978-1-908251-67-1

The author's right to be identified as author of this book under the
Copyright, Designs and Patents Act 1988 has been asserted.

Printed and bound in Poland

Cover design by Mark Mechan

Typeset by Park Productions

The publisher acknowledges subsidy towards
this publication from Creative Scotland

For further information on Vagabond Voices, see the website,
www.vagabondvoices.co.uk

for my mum and dad
Lorna M. Husband & Charles M.G. Husband

Contents

Extremely Large Telescope	3
The man on the corner of Sproul Plaza sold black holes	4
Co-ordinates	5
On being observed	6
Losing it	7
Of those that rise at night	8
Making sense	9
Everything you'd said to her	13
Behind the zoo	14
And one night	15
High tide	16
Community Liaison at Torness	17
Acts of sleep: four prologues	18
Still life	19
Adages for late flowering crones	20
Shipping Frika to Céret	21
Habitacle	22
Sylvia on Primrose Hill	23
The physics of a name	24
Inheritance	25
Miming the universe	26
The reading	27
The haar	28
Promise to the dog	29
Settling the creeks	30
As if Sunday morning, Loch Eribol	31
Advances	32
Top left: soundscape	33
Partnership at Langass, North Uist	34
Clocked	35
Post-punk idyll	36
High windows	37
A long held view	38
On retirement	39
Gobby	40
What do the horses think?	42

Little Sparta 43
Desire paths 44
Bird tongues 45
The Coppice Room 46
Still running 47
Australian sundials 48
Be my guest 49
Above the snow line 50
Giacca civetta / owl jacket 51
Slightly too accurate atomic time and the leap second 52
From Laetoli, in the rain 53
Eclipse 54
Superposition at ten 55
Reciting to the bees 56
Nostalgia 57
Jean's Theory of Everything 59
The End of the Stelliferous Era 61

Notes 63
Acknowledgements 67

This Far Back Everything Shimmers

Extremely Large Telescope

We listen at the door of the room,
the Universe has just made its grand
entrance, the energetic reception
flattens the walls, creates new dimensions.

A jazz band is getting ready to play
the next number, wiping spit
from its mouthpiece; expectation
has its own gravitational pull.

So this is a night, the first one, already
cooling. But the crowd still expanding, pushing out.

Light plays the darling, rumouring
through the crowd. We watch it shrink
to hear-say; histories glint in glass eyes.

The lone note of a trumpet drifts
down between the years, its wave and
bounce barely stirring the bluesy smoke.

This far back everything shimmers.
We must get here earlier next time, we say,
as the Universe milks faint applause.

The man on the corner of Sproul Plaza sold black holes

The man on the corner of Sproul Plaza sold black holes and real estate
on the moon. He got by, he said, from those who knew an opportunity
when they saw one. Couple of sales a month was enough to keep his kids
in shoes. He claimed there was a market out there for the unique,
and he had more stock than America could afford.

I stopped by every few weeks to see how many he'd sold, left just before
he put pen to paper. I wasn't interested in the moon, knew it would be crowded
before long, but the information paradox of black holes tempted my money.

After a while the man turned a deaf ear to my enquiries, smiled at passers-by
as I talked, not wasting his time on a waster like me. I pressed him as to how
I'd recognise one of his opportunities when I saw it. *You won't,* he said
truthfully, *until you pass the event horizon by which time it'll be too late.*
He eyed up a woman in bohemian clothes.

I wanted him to know I was no fool. I'd read up enough to ask what properties
I could expect, if I were to make a purchase. He locked my eye, sensing the scent
of a sale. *Only mass,* he said, *I can't guarantee angular momentum or electric charge.*

I bought it outright that day, sealed with a handshake. I still have the certificate
somewhere in the attic. The man's been gone a while now, and when I walk by
the empty pitch I think it would be crazy not to, with all that stock to sell.

Co-ordinates

In obsolete branches of the dark
co-ordinates of space are marked by birds –
small birds: finches, warblers, dunnocks
and the like, petrified in stellar spindrift,
wings tucked rigid, feet clutching
two tiny O's.

Inaccurate markers these but no matter.
No-one checks flock precision as they ring
and scatter. Or counts those absent
from their perch.

On being observed

When I woke up she asked me what I'd been smiling at
as I slept. Was it dachshunds? she said. No, I replied
I'm pretty sure it was a dream about organisational change
at work. The treads of the steps to our office grew narrower
and we all had to wear smaller shoes. But the smiling?
she asked. Oh, I was probably just being polite.

Losing it

She told me her brother lived in America for years and managed not to.
She reprimanded the tea, blew on it, looked out a window onto the backs
of tenements she grew up with, asked where we were in relation to home.

The kitchen looked strange, white and empty, she said. And why we only
had one pint of milk, and nothing else, seemed to worry her. All her life
she'd made it this way: boiled water, swirled the pot, emptied it, peered in.

The next time I met her, maybe three years later, she didn't remember
that conversation. Or when I'd taken her home to her flat and she waltzed
me round, gave me a biscuit that crumbled to dust when exposed to air.

This time she looked out a window onto a tree. Said my accent was clear
enough. Then we both sat watching my voice tremble on the tree. Each
small word faltered, came loose. We watched them fall, fall, then brown.

Of those that rise at night

Dwarfs balance on rubber-tipped chopsticks, step
in waltz-time: bedroom to bathroom to kitchen, mass
is spread over larger bones; on a coronal plane
each quiet collapse reveals more caverns; always
slightly smaller when they arrive, than when they left.

Subgiants get stuck in comfortable chairs, cradled
by unforgiving foam, work up a sweat that grows
fabulous microbial creatures. Skin pinks while
ischaeal tuberostities coorie into pillowy dermal
layers of cheeks, until they ruddy then black.

Normal giants can't fall back over, instead they rise
and flick the switch on a kettle, listen to it growl
into life. After it fades, the monstrous pelt of silence
returns. They sip tea, just to feel the kinks in their gut,
to imagine themselves in three dimensions.

Luminous giants stand at windows waxing gibbous
to full, their stare reflecting the love-sick light
back on itself, a menage-a-trois from sun to moon
to face. It feels as if no-one else is running tonight
in this three-legged race of wave and particle.

Less luminous supergiants, orbited by an oort cloud
of dead cells, hirple to the bathroom. They stare
at baby-toothed enamel. Sometimes a plughole yawns
and it's a mouth they could so easily fall into, gripping
the cold shoulders of the sink they stop themselves.

Most luminous supergiants struggle to lift oedematous legs
into single divans, spill over edges when they turn, cling
to cliffs of sleep. They lie on racks of electric blankets, roast
under winter togs, watch headlights roam across the ceiling.
They are a static centre; it's the rest of the universe that spins.

Making sense

i

The room was dark   save for her figure crooked
before a 32 inch telly and not a foot
from it   Macular
de-
gen-
eration and a hardness
of hearing meant
she had to get close to
        match words
she hadn't heard for years
like
      carriage
                  commoner and
                              Duchess
with
          pixels   of red
white and blue

ii

She asked *if I would*
rub liquid paraffin
into tinder-dry skin So I helped her off
with a slip set about lathering
the creased saddle of a
ninety-five-year-old back
She shivered and sighed
then watched as I swept up
  sequins of cells
                she'd cast
                        like
                    younger selves

iii

They fell from her
like teeth
  jumped ship
or were scrambled dead
in her mouth on arrival
fumbled misgivings
stems lobes and bowls uncoupled
then crisscrossed
put the brakes on sharpish
before they even breached
        even spat
d i s s o l v i n g   syllabub soft
foaming from high-flutes
        beyond her
but she pickled when she heard

iv

It's anyone's guess now
which night stemmed
which day Among the papers
of my life a sheer volume
of light is pressed sprung
with ascenders & descenders
of foliage soon to frame
the hair's breadth of me

And to remember is to
core-sample a seam to find
half-lives in the jostle
and decay When I read
the diary of my mind it's chalk
on white pages a crush
of bones Here I stand small
beside the high cliff of my years

Everything you'd said to her

As her daughter, I was sure she knew
the shapes of my mouth well enough
to make an educated guess.

But you, the one she had called
softly spoken, were quiet that day
we drove across from the West

to see her for the first time since
she'd had them fitted. Worried
in fact that you might be asked

to repeat everything you'd said
to her in the past eight years.

Behind the zoo

A zebra stopped my father in his tracks, going up
Corstorphine Hill. Always reluctant to break stride
with his into-a-strong-wind-even-on-a-calm-day walk
he will have stuttered to a halt. I imagine the split

second when he thinks, where am I? Before remembering
the hill rises behind the zoo. I picture the green
of my father's eyes, the shadow of fence wire portioning
his face. And the zebra cantering off towards the city.

And one night

Who'd have thought the Arabian Sea would be like this: flat packed,
labelled like a life-vest, tucked under the fuselage? But up here they deal
in miniatures – life's accoutrements shrunk, gift-wrapped then thrown
into a hidey-hole. We're transported chair-shaped, watch stories of clouds
through pantry-sized windows; heads resting on dolls' pillows we eat,
from teddy bear bowls, food that is both welcome and tasteless.

The default music is Springsteen, insistent that although everything dies
it may all come back. And – as the plane staccatos across a rudimentary
drawing of a landscape, as the air outside is surely solid at minus 85 degrees –
we see the glittering Arabian is soon to be consumed by an obverse world
of darkness, which we in our chairs hope to outrun, fast-forwarding ourselves
into tomorrow before we're ready, before breakfast.

High tide

Nearing the high tide mark of midsummer my knowledge of darkness shrinks
as I go to bed at a childish time awaken at four to – what I've learnt is –
nautical dawn awaken again brightly at five just to conclude
my knowledge of sunlight is similarly half-baked

Watching a gold-leaf moth realise the wider world
(after an all-you-can-eat buffet of winter wool) I wonder if I'm sleeping
through my life   caught in a well-lit imitation of summer while summer has in fact
declared its independence from the other seasons and is basking somewhere off shore

Community Liaison at Torness

For two days now the reactor has been shut off and staff sit waiting
for local trawlers to net the blooms of jellyfish. As yet, there's no
explanation for such a furore on the Berwickshire coastline. Jellyfish
crowd around a seawater filter, garlanded with wrack and jostling
with placards of wood, carrying faded names of fishing ports
and brands of whisky.

It's as if hundreds of hippies have been reincarnated and flash-mob
the waters. Linking tentacles, the pale moons of their bodies bond
together. The plant sends Community Liaison to smooth things over –
she shouts into a loud-hailer a testament of safety stats and naturally
occurring forms of radiation, sings the praises of reprocessing
in millisieverts, terabecquerels.

After a while the jellyfish seem to get the gist of half-life, communing
with the voice on a far-out wavelength. Some drift off on the trail
of zooplankton. Others shout from their frilly mouths: *Wait, come back
there's strength in numbers.* But they're rudderless in an ocean current
like peregrinators at the mercy of a god. Or a diligent rent-a-mob
moving on, other causes to champion.

Acts of sleep: four prologues

Act I
In which you avoid the insomniac's eye using synaptic tricks to deflect
it's gaze; ignore hear-say (it is contagious); down tisanes of chamomile,
skim shale-thin thoughts over sleep's meniscus until your mind is
suspended – like noctilucent cloud or damsel-fly – above its surface.

Act II
In which the one you're looking for is quick as equatorial nightfall, slips
from moorings, has the grip of undertow, the strength of concrete after
years of curing, it breaches all banks of the body until legs – plumbed
with lead – concede to the athleticism of sleep, its sudden victory.

Act III
In which you prepare for delays as you're held fast, bound to the spindle
of sleep's mast, thalassa-sick with temporary paralysis, ears stoppered
with beeswax to the ambient world, and to a fickle flock of obligations
that appear as a murmuration through the dusk of your falling.

Act IV
In which hours are lost to this chartless place, only waves are traced, night
is scuppered by daybreak; some return with a periplous logged in memory:
the wrath of a coast, safe harbour, archipelagos of narwhals tusking
in ice floes; all dreams must be smuggled from the wreck of your waking.

Still life

Still life in front of a balcony by Louis Marcoussis, 1928

Waves have been saved from the sea!
Plucked out, they are rather shapely
their statistics are 36, 28, 34

A fulsome jug is balanced, as we are,
a little awkwardly on a
potbellied man-do-lin

The mandolin mouth is shaping up
to make a sound, strung
with three h o r i z o n s that catch
like fishing line in its throat

Three bars that keep repeating are:
pa-pa-pum
pa-pa-pum
pa-pa-pum

Through the open balcony door we see
the brink of a view –
a beach promenades past

And all the while a sardine flushes red,
framed on a plate, mouth agape, it waits
to receive the water that is just about to tip
from the jug

Shadows are cut patterns, ready
to be made into suits

There is a hesitation
in the floor, table, pressed light and ceiling

Look out! The sky is wood grain

Adages for late flowering crones

after Leonora Carrington

Ways of looking intently involve holding your eye on a stick or
frying it, wide and yellow-irised, puddled at the edges.

Huddle around and crowdfund your ideas of how a flower
could break through paving that yesterday was its ceiling.

Wait long enough and your once limestone face will meta-
morphose into marble streaked like a painting of fat rich meat.

The gunnels of you may be be overrun by children with sharp
toenails, shrieking like parrots; you've no need to embrace this.

Avoid stepping on the cracks in the faces of other old ladies;
they'll be more accepting of you if you dress like them in crow-skins.

Stand beside a mature tree to remind your skeleton of the work
it has to do; a hunch may be a memory of apples it once bore.

Most cats these days keep an implacable cut-out of themselves
and sit behind it keeking through opaline apertures.

By now you should have mistressed a masque of disinterest; it is
with regret I must inform you, there's much to be learned from cats.

When the ends of the day meet is when coffee is most likely to stain
your teeth, rivering fissures in the enamel, ox-bowing tiny lakes.

Climbing a ziggurat is invariably ominous. Beware also of lagging
behind your shadow; shadows with eye-holes; turning any shade blue.

Detective work is well suited to ageing rapunzels. Enhance your chances
by wearing a fedora, sooking a pipe, carrying your burdens in clear view.

It works two ways: pipe smoke contemplates your alveoli, breaches
its branches, finding you out. However, in reality the only way out is:

a cowhorn handle-barred bicycle. It can wait nonchalantly, all day and
the dropped crossbar is ridable in crow-skins. The flower is a decoy.

Shipping Frika to Céret

from Picasso's letters, 1912

First, send the dog. Then my brushes
dirty and clean, my palettes, stretchers,
canvas, stencils and metal comb
(for the *faux bois*), linen, blankets, bolsters,
my kimono with the yellow flowers;
tubes of paint: white ivory, black,
burnt sienna, greens – emerald and Verona,
ultramarine, Peruvian ochre, umber,
vermillion, cadmiums – yellow and dark;
a bottle of siccative, packets of charcoal.

Madame Pichot has the cats, the monkey;
hang a *for rent* at the Bateau Lavoir.

Habitacle

Le Corbusier's favourite chair was a cockpit seat Inspired by functionality
he observed how smart aeronautical design could lend itself to pure living
space He saw elegance in the purr of a white shape an arc of air fluming
a wing a rendered wall bisecting   blue sky
In the same way he considered   the spirit
departing the body   as a controlled ascent

Sylvia on Primrose Hill

I hear the seals bark in summer time, in the zoo
on the hill, the yellow hill
I live on.

The seals bark like pets I keep at the far end
of the garden. I don't have to feed them
or pet them

but I know they're here with me, on the yellow hill,
barking. I hear them. But they have no idea
that I do.

The physics of a name

for Milo

Your earliest likeness: an abstract twin
you quickly became and which became you.

This sigh shaped itself as a call you knew
to answer. Its high-low, sing-song sound

you take with you wherever you go. Soon
you'll give it out, the first part of yourself

to give, and when you do you'll learn the ways
it can be spoken, cried and thrown, you'll learn

what *sotto voce* means, and un-said. Then,
once you've calculated the mass of sound,

you'll find you know its gravity, its pull.

Inheritance

My mother makes a joke of it
telling me she searched all day
unable to find the damn thing
after taking it off to do the dishes, irritated
whenever she glanced at her wrist for the time.

Only at night when undressing for bed
she discovers it, on her other wrist.

Miming the universe

She smoothes an invisible tablecloth, both hands flat
stretching out in each direction, then gathers arms
around an imaginary friend or beach ball.
Seeing blank faces, she scoops a saddle shape
from air, one plummet of a rollercoaster.
They make stupid guesses until someone shouts:
Just tell us what it is.
She runs outside, spins herself dizzy, lays down.
They gaze through the patio door then, bored
go back to their drinks. She's pinned to the ground
grass grows slowly beneath her, smokers step over her.
She watches for a tell-tale crease in the supple sky.

The reading

Not knowing you, this uninvited vantage
of the back of your head feels like trespass.

I can't help but see your hairs, close-cut and clean,
whorl their fingerprint around your crown. Light

draws each stem of the crop. Each has the intimacy
of a thought, silvering the bowl of your head.

I notice too, a flatness where your parietal-occipital
skull bones meet. As if as a child you lay too long looking up at the sky.

The haar

        hangs low, ceiling
to the sky, it will hang
all day. Outside is roomed in
a landscape tight and small
the haar pressing down
on all beneath it, birds even
unable to rise up, weighted
to fences, wires, roofs.

The puffy damp sits
on shoulders, neck, crown;
my brain is dew fangled wool.
With no wind to blow
these thoughts away
they pile up in cramped air
moulding into a mood
the out-of-order sky
won't let loose.

Promise to the dog

When you die, I tell him, I'll dissolve
all your organs except for your heart,
wash your insides with wine, lay you out
for forty days in sunlight and salt.
I'll print strips of linen with spells, call
to the gods in prayer as you're tightly bound
in diamonds and squares. I'll mask your snout,
paint kohl rimmed eyes, preserve solemnity
in that expression of yours. You'll sit, wait
until the boats are built and moored
underground, provisions of meat cured,
parcelled. You yawn, unaware of the weight
of a heart, a feather; your tongue un-scrolls
like a book, I read your clean, pink soul.

Settling the creeks

Drive me down creek
Drive me rock and pillow
Drive me raggedy, rough, slip-sliding creek
Drive me late creek
Drive me mist-lifting-early
Drive me deep shit
Drive me gorgéd and tidal
Drive me little hou hou
Drive me

Drive me to the pan rattles
til fern-dripping-palm-stinky, rib-eyed and cow-crazy
to glitterburn

If I go gold-fielding to nugget creek
or greenstone bent for the old pounamu
then call my bluff creek

Drive me dismal, drive me dizzy, drive me half way
Drive me roaring swine to goat prospecting
to pommel, peculiar and punchbowl
Drive me old ma

Drive me solitude to the firewood
to leaning rock and mutton town
Drive me thirsty, shingle, chasm, caution, fork and broken
and moonlight creek

Drive me boundary creek to judge creek
Drive me gunboat, slaughterhouse
and lonely grave

Drive me back of beyond creek
tell me how I got here creek
to where I'm from

As if Sunday morning, Loch Eribol

Only today I understand, with a morning as still
as this, how it could all seem created. Nothing moves
in the sky – not a plane, a cloud – a hawk sits dazed
in a field, as if dropped; submarines ghost the loch.

This hour is an implausible world, as if the natural
order of things is suspended for maintenance –
and I can only watch, with a taxidermist's eye,
as a diorama of a day is curated before me.

Advances

Spring advances its army faster now than a hundred years ago, mobilising
troops of hawthorn flowers, orange-tipped butterflies, an arrow-shower
of swallows at a sprightly average of 1.9 miles per hour, South to North
up the British Isles.

While in benign-blue skies: two jets exercise. As I run, they run cross-
country, grazing the horizon, one spearhead follows another
as flint, obsidian, chert.

The North waits patiently for the fastest Hermès to arrive – just one ladybird
is enough, then three weeks of rioting skies, of wing and blossom, before
a frog finally spawns on Shetland and winter can be declared
defeated once more.

Hand shading my eyes I enjoy the simple spectacle. And isn't it funny how
we know that sound lags behind light, but find it hard to look ahead
when our own ears deceive us.

Top left: soundscape

But heft that stone. It has a language beyond our hearing.
— Norman MacCaig

For the silence but
to hear my heart's bass beat slow
to the pace of permafrost to hear magnetism
from the poles as a tuning fork a slur
of tide in the glottal stop of a rock pool   waves groom
the space between sands' chittering teeth   tongues
blacken into bands of mica-schist
silence become hirsute
but silence recruits an ensemble of air
clouds rink the sky gulls ride a shanty
of a breeze feathers greased to its tune heat complains
as it climbs from the earth
a crepitus of light falls crooked as phalanges
silence warms-up instruments out-of-kilter
dusk flexes a bruising musculature
the ocean floor vents curses magma blisters
like mulligatawny Later stars come out
with a compositional debut shimmy
in a little black number their lonesome *shooby-doos* break the law
every night to sing through
the near-perfect vacuum of space

Partnership at Langass, North Uist

for Kirstie and Marianne

Round here things like love
are kept in a cist on a hill weighted
with basalt dolerite camptonite
moated by peat-gold water a ring
of bracken bog asphodel heather

Round here the ancients sit
in circles are remembered daily
in a name a song Their hearts
are chambered like ours

Round here land is hand-tooled
dug with wrack and tang
Time is grown exchanged
you only have to ask

Tides are watched like a clock

In winter breath is counted

We saw you coming a long way off
a hard crossing waves like blades
But you're here now

Sit yourselves down

Clocked

I clocked you at the bar:
gnomon of a mohawk,
ring glint in your lower lip.
The proverbial two hands
flitting over that fraction
of night doesn't express
the other dimensions:
of luck, of the relative
space-time co-ordinates
of my friends, you choosing
to stay for just one more.
And moreover, my usually
reticent self, springing to the bar
to ply you with conversation
and later, pull you by the hand
into the orbit of this dance.

Post-punk idyll

Savages score the road from Tongue to Sangobeg as diesel burns up
the Moine Thrust, bass guitar reverbs along Eribol, glisters off mica
off feldspar. Then Camille's voice starts low, throws itself as echolalia
in chambered cairns, swallows me like a soutterain, slides from iliac crest
to symphysis and arch of bone, frets the teeth of greening skulls sunk
in bracken beds. Camille, drumming up the headland, insists: *she will she will she will*
as pink quartzite seams give it up to vanishing point, chords thrum
with bellowed breath; beyond here a carboniferous swamp exhales
where the carapaces of a billion creatures lie spent under a heft
of years; and a long drag of road rises and cools in the rear view.

High windows

At the top of the mainland's most northerly mountain, with boggy puddles frozen
into craquelure, and a view of the North Atlantic looking blue, I receive a sales call:
triple glazing is being offered with quality polyurethanes and a ten year guarantee.
I smell the air, snow buntings fly-by Red Arrows style, sunlight grazes in the glen,
clouds skiff over Eribol. I want to share it with the caller, tell him to leave his desk
and walk out of the industrial estate into whatever nature he can find –traffic island,
verge, lone tree rupturing a pavement– and embrace it. But it's a recorded message.

A long held view

At the last moment it
hesitates/ or rather
we do/ to brace
a small part of ourselves
which still believes in
certainty/ suspend
a long held view of skylines
that dates back to
the longevity of hills/
anticipating foundations
being rocked we rush
to shock-absorb the soul/
and when the razing starts
it's thankfully slow/ as if
to let us down gently/ first
air warm as eggs casts
its heat/ rooms release
their light/ the shell creaks
a little before sky rivers
in/ a cloud of dust mush-
rooms up like proving
dough/ concrete gives
a grunt then the whole
falters/ apologetic almost
before sauntering apart/
pictures of pop stars &
dogs & green ladies jump
their frames/ calendars slip
from pins loosing a hive
of empty boxes/ ceiling roses
impress into laminate boards
weighted by twenty floors flat-
packing themselves walls de-
fenestrating doors slammed thin
and a rain of nails prised free
from soft beds makes sweet
timpani with concrete slabs
and all the iron knitting unravels
like storeys like storeys like stories

of moonlight
the commute
to catch
mile gap
million
a quarter
(on average)
that mind
shifting eyes
by night-
travelled
distance
the same
and back
to the moon
distance as
the same
travelled
escalator
this old
notice:
just a
engraved
no watch
no fuss
no cake

On retirement

Gobby

Ah wis the gobby
wan in the yard banged oan
aboot oor rights

fir thirty year aw
that fight got naewhere fast
then it closed like

aw the rest Only
later they found the 'sbestos
stowed away in

ma lungs smuggling
ma breath oot leaving me
little tae go on

The ships Ah built up
knocked me doon in the end
First the cough cough cough

then quickening breath
til ony lang sentence wis
scuppered by wheezing

The wife squanders her
breath on the fags but no here
wi the oxygen

that could blow us aw
tae smithereens Ah couldnae
dae withoot it noo

Ah need it jist tae
dae the daftest o things
It's like pitting on

ma sock pause sock pause
shoe pause shoe Cannae go far
Ah'm like a dug on

a lead or wean with
its umbilical cord
a circle like they

say from cradle to
y'know But Ah'm planning ma
escape jist brooding

o'er the detail
Ah've become the quiet
type nae longer talk

shite cannae afford
tae Ah'm a man o measured
words near poetic

The wife says Ah talk
in haikus Can you no jist
gimme peace wuman?

Ah beg of her on
wan o those airless summer
nights when ahm

lying wi the ship
on tap o me breathing in
the coal black sea She

has no reply Her
grey eyes treading water
watch me slowly drown

What do the horses think?

What do the horses think
on a Saturday night in Glasgow, walking
the trough-like alleys, shadows saddled
with luminous riders? Drawing the city
in draughts through their nostrils, they sift
for the heat of crime, the creature-scent
of humans, the reek of waste. Ears swivel
to catch the lone song of a drunk, wild call
of the pack, first tremor of a stampede.

Passers-by may think
they've imagined these shapes, or conjured
them from the past; horse-shoes ringing
on cobbles echo off steel-trees, vertical lakes
of glass. Do they fantasise of clover fields,
nose-bags, blue skies and sweated miles;
or later, safely stabled, will they re-live
the night: steering a baying crowd
into sticky pens, ghost-drawn carriages?

Little Sparta

I glimpse you between gaps in the trees: flammable,
blue, longing to be lit. We walk the garden separately

meet-up at its ponds, stare into their travelled faces,
hold hands in the woods. I trip over words that riddle

the paths. They guide us round, past Apollo's golden head,
we pay homage then are led, politely, back to the gate.

The distant hills are fixtures, like old aunts. Summer has flitted,
Autumn rummages in the abandoned wealth; before long

it will all be spent. And we'll be rattling like winter shadows,
warming our hands on a bonfire of things not set in stone.

Desire paths

Ad astra per aspera

As town planners will tell you the way the heart takes you won't be on road
won't be on pavement or well lit or even signposted. More likely for it to wear
a shy track, flattening stems of spring grass to a darker, muddied green, clipping
a corner of a verge, jay-walking across places that don't have a name: nettled ground
moating a nail house shuttered by day, a gap through fly-tipped debris, balding weeds
that hold up a wall shark-finned with glass then under a strip of trees no-one bothers
to own. Eventually all ways converge on the edge of town, where land stretches
to wide horizon, where every desire path reaches for its vanishing point
before heading off to shortcut a rumoured route between the stars.

Bird tongues

in a wood panelled back room drawers
are lined with bird skins: a neat flock
filed in rows of holotype, wings folded
flat, feet tied with string, labelled, eyes
stitched shut. But two beaks left ajar

so bird tongues wag

tell tales of blossom that smelt like
rotten meat, insects that fought back
or weighed them down dangerously
low, winds seeded with gunshot, birds
disappearing into flower heads

swallowed whole like a song

The Coppice Room

after Andy Goldsworthy

He framed the wood with an invitation
– a doorway cut from one of his own –
and contained it like a parfumier or husband
so I couldn't not walk in. Immediately I ranked
among the trees, their tall limbless bodies
un-limbed me. Then further in, beyond the reach
of breadcrumbed light, I fell a mile down into
an ocean, out of the sun's depth, a mile below
the crust of the earth, a slim stratum. Here trees
stood closer together so I was hard pushed to
squeeze between the trunks, knocked shoulders
elbows knees against the dark trying to figure it out.
I struggled less, slowed to a stop, found myself, arms
tight to my sides, deep in this roomed wood, held.

Still running

She didn't know what had become of the memory,
was reluctant when he'd asked, digging down
with his words. But there was something in the forest
that once was a swamp. Good conditions *apparently*:
anoxic, mud covered. She leafed through stone books,
split open shale pages, wondered over the blue-grey
and blank. Then suddenly a pygmy horse still running –
chalk skeleton, berries constellated in an obsolete belly.

Australian sundials

The equation of time is the same/ Our sun moves from East to
West in all cases/ Our celestial pole is North in the Northern
hemisphere South in the Southern hemisphere/ When
a gnomon points to the equator that means North in
the Southern hemisphere South in the Northern
hemisphere/ Shadows fall just the same but
move anti-clockwise/ We have passed our
meridian/ As your children grow long
and begin to marry/ our parents
shorten on the other side of
the globe/ unable now
to circle it

Be my guest

You're welcome to use my bath anytime.
I've heard you talk of the now inadequate one
in your new-built home, and how you lie
with knees bent or breasts resting on
the water's surface, like an ancient landscape;
shoulders a raised beach, far from shore.

Be my guest. This tub of antique metal
(lion's feet at the front, pipe at the back,
grappling taps, a knob marked *waste* to pull
the plug) has ample room for your burgeoning
curves, and is beyond the needs of my frame.
I rarely use it; it takes so long to fill. Instead
I shower standing – a mast on a dry-docked boat.

I'll run it now, close over the door until tiles
trickle, water swallows up all but your head
and crannog of belly. Close your eyes, and feet
will carry you off, fur soaking steam, claws
ticking. Slide your ear beneath the membrane
and listen to blood finding the maze of you.
Hear it – pa-Pum, pa-Pum – caving your hearts.

Above the snow line

Only the sun climbs with me
no birds this year even buntings
absent just blinter to catch
the eye a frazilled wind scrape
of boots on rimed rock daggers
of ice dreeping over outcrops
gravity and my weight
compressing a jillion
spearheaded snowflakes

This desire to be uppermost
most Northerly highest
hereabouts the first today
to print a long unscripted
prayer is vanity no doubt
but also a tuning out a yearly
pilgrimage to the ice-house
of my mind   world temporarily
held under dust sheets

Or a tuning in to white noise
bone-creak from the great beyond
louder up here in proximity
to the ghosts and gods that orbit
our black socket of sky No use looking
for them through anti-glare instead
I reach out well perfused fingers
to un-give the messages they leave
frosted in braille

Giacca civetta / owl jacket

– a jacket placed on the back of a chair in an office to indicate the owner's presence at work when they are in fact gallivanting elsewhere

Sometimes, we both perform
an act of presenteeism
in our conversation: eyes engaging
while our minds swivel 270 degrees
in the treetops. Yours (ironically) on work,
the vagaries thereof, closing the pay gap
or not. And mine on some metaphor
that flew into my head then perched
in a dark corner, observable only by the sound
of readjusted feathers. In the background
your *chat* – on hegemony, heteronormity
and other terms that bounce off
the flat dish of my face – reaches the peak
of its pique as I am hunting a vole, hovering
with intent above the forest floor when
–in response to some hyper-sonic cue–
I tune back into you and stare
yellow-lamped, shuffling eyelids
like screen-wipers, quite unaware
what has been said. Slowly, I drop
porcelain bones, spit a mouthful
of fur, take that old jacket from the back
of my chair, and redress.

Slightly too accurate atomic time *and the leap second*

It's never a showy release
No floodlit stadium whooping crowd
gate lifting to loose
spindly dogs powered
by brindled legs and hunger
But more discreet
More rumour and look
the other way as a flea
– chosen for *acrobatic prowess* –
– hailed as *The nimblest this circus has ever known* –
is unleashed then lost
in a flicker and a blink
And we're left with tales
of leaping a hundred times its own height
tightrope walking a line of atoms
lifting hours with its teeth dressed only
in a hat and fur stole witnessed
by a man in Beijing and proven
by pages of numbers and symbols
that from a distance resemble
footfalls in snow Meanwhile *we're told*
caesium clocks carry on
unerringly

From Laetoli, in the rain

Still a wonder: this arch
vaulted in ligament
tendon plantar fascia
propelling a hirsute
bipedal ancestor
through the pliocene
to us

Imprinting a layer
of volcanic ash
heel-strikes mark
each sole next to
rain drops cuneiforms
of bird feet and hyena
hipparion boar

All out on excursions
when captured for three
and a half million years
before erosion again
revealed them
forever-walking
into a distant present

Eclipse

i.m. Alexander Hutchison

I observe it on an empty road outshining
an alignment of sodium-suns that caramelise
the small hours
Tonight is foxed by this supermoon sky
It casts me as a long hand over
a dial of room:
I climb a ladder of floorboards strum spines
on the bookshelf shiver
like a black flame in the grate then gather
with others in creases
and craters And when all that is left lit
is a glimmering rim of coin it flips
like grief turns tangible
a coppery sob on the tongue
We absorb mostly blue light so what falls
into our umbra – Storms Tranquility Nectar –
blazes
before normal service is resumed,
the moon cut and pasted in a screensaver sky
By morning it will be goose-grey
and leaving
to winter elsewhere

Superposition at ten

as polling stations close on the night of the Scottish Independence referendum 2014

We are decided yet undeclared
we are cast and reeled in
we are rains and we are frogs
we are bees and frost
we are captured and released
we are being counted
we have never been so convinced
we are held and upheld
we are suspended in aspic jellied disbelief
we are buttered and rejected
we are hectored and complex
we are mining and striking
we are ready to be induced
we are missile and target
we are jet propelled we are ocean-going we are land-based
we are a labour of love
we have an oxygen saturation rate of 97%
we are five point three million odd and one
we are descendants of fish

Reciting to the bees

At the NHS Apiary I make a prophylactic appointment, and am told a drowsy summer is their busy time. Once checked-in, I leaf through wildlife magazines before being called into clinic: a sterile room with an illusion of trees on the facing wall. I'm asked to relax in a chair as a bowl of bees are placed over my head, ventilated glass separates the swarm from my mouth, my breath given a chance to manifest before them. The bees' Pavlovian responses are put to the test: trained to detect a whiff of cancer corrupting a cell, proboscises dip the air expecting sugar-water reward if anything is amiss, humming while they work in the downdraft of my sighs. I recite Yeats, as my face hovers in their glade. And the bees hang on my every word, hungry for the scent of malignancy.

Nostalgia

Remember how we sat on that small rock, polishing our glass eyes,
fields of ears pricked, fishing an ebbing tide for *anybody-out-there?*
We counted waves flat-lining our shore. Took us a while to castaway.
But still we look up after dark. And still we steer by obituaries of light.

Jean's Theory of Everything

She asks them to leave the door open and from her bed calls
the garden in. A brash wind is the first guest bringing a party
of others: soil, leaves that frill the skirting, smells and rubbish
make themselves at home. The roof gives up, lets the rain join in
and through frail panes the sun sits a while, empty handed.

Slugs traipse all night across her floor. She thinks they're fat
and what a waste of time making a marathon trip only to be burst
by the beaks of birds, to slouch to sticky puddles. Seeds scatter
themselves like poor punctuation, taking root in the rug. Soon
green shoots poke through, and worms doing morning yoga.

By winter the lens of her eye has a coating of ice, giving her
a convex gaze. Now she can see the microcosm of things:
parasites living on the hairs of mice, and the architecture
of skin. Nature is a grafter, she grants it that, its work
cut out just keeping tabs on all those leptons and quarks.

She feels much better when gravity lifts, like a hospital blanket
it was too heavy and not very warm. On discovering she is curled
around other dimensions, her vertigo disappears and it explains
that recent trouble with word search. She's also comforted to learn
her tinnitus was actually Cosmic Microwave Background.

Jean networks with dark matter and finds him to be a nice chap
holding down a job. She has yet to meet dark energy but no wonder,
the expansion of the universe is a thankless task. She can empathise
with this as she moved house many times before her fifth child
was born. Then Jim had the op and the extension was built.

Now she's on the Nomenclature Committee, as the physicists lacked
an adult approach. She feels like the Queen every time a quantum
discovery sails off with the title she gives it. Inspirations include
martial arts and founding members of the W.I. She considers her other
poor selves working in dead-end jobs in alternate universes.

At night she could watch the nebulae for hours. She prefers them
to soaps and feigns shock as they sow their stellar seed into space as if
it never happened in her day. Constellations flick past like an album
of old photographs; she reminisces about light when it was young.
It is around this time Jean conceives her Theory of Everything.

The End of the Stelliferous Era

Do not look up   light is exhausted
                    Lag your body in wool   dark
amassing quickly now   wind up, until
unsustainable   finite resources have peaked   Stamp!
Sing elegies!   like a rush to the head   before our sun folds black
                                    deletions corroborate
             stretch languorously   Tie yourself to a chair,
                        across an un-unified verse   Maths
can be a great distraction   waves longer than
the observable   What-was-once hacked
                    now functionally extinct   Morse code;
no expletives please   assemble
                        the last of the wine, a reasonable fee
             formerly luminous become cold and faint
if astrology is your guiding light   the longest living are of
low mass   personality loss may occur
          with every   Green being the first to deplete
a paucity   stock-piled vitamin D
colliding in dim   strewn   Later,
occasional brown dwarfs   Take time to consider your nearest ex
                                    candle some far corner,
may be light years behind you
                        dissipating
take an umbrella from under your seat, in the event of
                                    at which point we'll know
particular decay.   A crushing sensation
                                                                      be succinct.
                        if the more advanced burn
time to inflate   us, bacteria
                                    and float
on a sea of cooling photons
                                                          the remains of day

Notes

The man on the corner of Sproul Plaza sold black holes
John Barrow in his book *Cosmic Imagery: Key Images in the History of Science (2008)* reports there was a street trader who stood on the corner of Sproul Plaza at Berkley University, California, selling black holes and real estate on the moon.

Community Liaison at Torness
In June 2011 Torness nuclear power station in East Lothian was shut down for two days due to large numbers of jellyfish found in sea water entering the plant.

Still life
The cubist painting *Still life in front of a balcony* by Louis Marcoussis hangs in The Kelvingrove Museum in Glasgow. This poem was written for a project on ekphrastic poetry linked to a conference run by Strathclyde University in 2013, with thanks to David Kinloch.

Shipping Frika to Céret
The poem takes phrases from letters sent by Pablo Picasso to his agent August Kahnweiler and his friend Georges Braques in 1912. *Faux bois* literally means false wood, an effect used by Picasso and Braque in their paintings.

Miming the universe
According to NASA the geometry of the universe could be positively curved like the surface of a sphere or negatively curved like the surface of a saddle, but the simplest version of inflationary theory, an extension of the Big Bang theory, predicts that the geometry of the universe is flat, like a sheet of paper.
http://map.gsfc.nasa.gov/universe/uni_shape.html [Accessed 2 July 2010].

Top left: soundscape
The quote is from Norman MacCaig's poem *Sounds and silences*. 'Top left' refers to the top left hand corner of the British Isles – Sutherland. A landscape that MacCaig spent much time in and wrote about extensively.

On retirement
'This escalator travelled the same distance as to the moon and back' was found written on a notice in Bank underground station, London, during its refurbishment.

Little Sparta
Ian Hamilton Findlay's garden, Little Sparta, is in South Lanarkshire.

Desire paths
Per aspera ad astra: latin for 'a rough road leads to the stars' or, as translated in Harper Lee's *To Kill a Mocking Bird*, 'From the mud to the stars'.

The Coppice Room
This artwork by Andy Goldsworthy can be found in Jupiter Artlands, West Lothian.

Slightly too accurate **atomic time and the leap second**
Since 1972, 26 leap seconds have been added to co-ordinated universal time; the last one was added on on 30th June 2015. This is to account for the difference between the slightly irregular rate of the earth's rotation and atomic time which is constant.

From Laetoli, in the rain
At Laetoli, Tanzania in 1978 tracks were excavated to reveal fossilised human footprints dating back 3.7 millions years. At the time they were the earliest example of early humans walking with a bi-pedal 'human-like' gait. Casts of the footprints are on display in museums around the world.

Superposition at ten
In quantum mechanics superposition describes the phenomenon whereby particles are thought to exist in different states at once until they are observed or measured.

Reciting to the bees
Honey bees have a powerful sense of smell and scientific experiments have successfully trained bees to detect different odours including disease. Designer Susana Soares produced a series of glass devices to facilitate bees interacting with a person's breath and allow them to indicate the presence of a specific odour.

Jean's Theory of Everything
In physics a 'unifying theory', or a 'theory of everything', that will accurately describe the universe on both a very large and very small scale, has yet to be found.

Acknowledgements

Thanks to the editors of the journals in which some of these poems first appeared: *fourfold, Gutter, Iota, Northwords Now, Magma, Smiths Knoll, The Rialto, The SHOp, Tears in the Fence, Under the Radar*. 'Gobby' won a runners-up prize in the inaugural Edwin Morgan International poetry prize 2009 and was first published in *Quill to Quark*, (Fleming publications). 'Extremely Large Telescope' was placed second in the Buchan poetry prize at Glasgow University 2010. A short selection of these poems was awarded a runners-up prize in the Pighog/Poetry School pamphlet competition, 2013. Thanks are due to my mentor on the Clydebuilt poetry apprenticeship scheme, the late great Alexander Hutchison, as well as others who provided valued feedback along the way: Maggie Rabatski, Ellen McAteer, Suzanne Motherwell, and poetry doulas, Mark Russell and Kathrine Sowerby. Special thanks to Jim Carruth whose labour of love – St. Mungo's Mirrorball network of Glasgow poets – is a source of support and inspiration.

Acknowledgements

Series editor: Colin Waters